Oceans
and Skies

by

Fran Sammis

BENCHMARK BOOKS

MARSHALL CAVENDISH
NEW YORK

Marshall Cavendish Corporation
99 White Plains Road
Tarrytown, New York 10591-9001

© Marshall Cavendish Corporation 2000

Series created by Blackbirch Graphics, Inc.

Printed in Hong Kong

Photo Credits
Page 22: ©F. Stuart Westmorland/Photo Researchers, Inc.; page 24: ©Fred McConnaughey/Photo Researchers, Inc; page 31: ©Charles Peale, H. Velten/ North Wind Picture Archives; page 33: ©Francois Gohier/Photo Researchers, Inc.; pages 35 and 36: ©PhotoDisc; page 42: ©NASA Science Source/Photo Researchers, Inc.; page 43: ©Luke Dodd, Science Photo Library/Photo Researchers, Inc.; page 57: ©Royal Observatory, Edinburgh-AATB-Science Photo Library/Photo Researchers, Inc; page 60: © Julian Baum, Science Photo Library/Photo Researchers, Inc.

Library of Congress Cataloging-in-Publication Data

Sammis, Fran
    Oceans and skies / by Fran Sammis
        p.   cm. — (Mapping our world)
    Includes bibliographical references and index.
    Summary: Explains how we have come to a better understanding of our planet by studying and mapping its oceans and the night sky above it.
        ISBN 0-7614-0374-4
        1. Oceanography—Juvenile literature. 2. Ocean—Juvenile literature. 3. Outer space—Exploration—Juvenile literature. [1. Oceanography. 2. Ocean. 3. Outer space—Exploration.] I. Title. II. Series: Sammis, Fran. Mapping our world.
    GC21.5 .S24   2000
    551.46—dc21   98-40835
                                                                                    CIP
                                                                                    AC

Contents

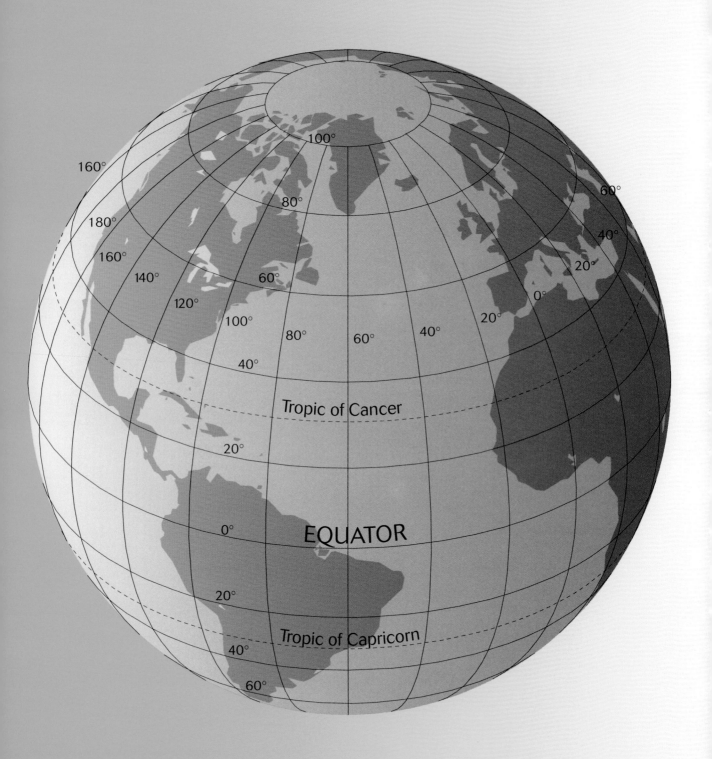

The Importance of Maps

As tools for understanding and navigating the world around us, maps are an essential resource. Maps provide us with a representation of a place, drawn or printed on a flat surface. The place that is shown may be as vast as the solar system or as small as a neighborhood park. What we learn about the place depends on the kind of map we are using.

Kinds of Maps

Physical maps show what the land itself looks like. These maps can be used to locate and identify natural geographic features such as mountains, bodies of water, deserts, and forests.

Distribution maps show where something can be found. There are two kinds of distribution maps. One shows the range or area a feature covers, such as a map showing where grizzly bears live or where hardwood forests grow.

The second kind of distribution map shows the density of a feature. That is, how much or how little of the feature is present. These maps allow us to see patterns in the way a feature is distributed. Rainfall and population maps are two examples of this kind of distribution map.

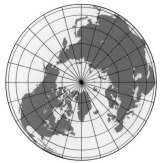

Globular

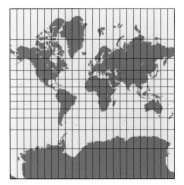

Mercator

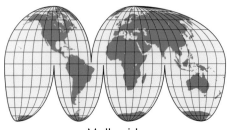

Mollweide

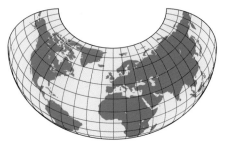

Armadillo

Political maps show us how an area is divided into countries, states, provinces, or other units. They also show where cities and towns are located. Major highways and transportation routes are also included on some kinds of political maps.

Movement maps help us find our way around. They can be road maps, street maps, and public transportation maps. Special movement maps called "charts" are used by airplane or boat pilots to navigate through air or on water.

Why Maps Are Important

Many people depend on maps to do their jobs. A geologist, for example, uses maps of Earth's structure to locate natural resources such as coal or petroleum. A transportation planner will use population maps to determine where new roads may need to be built.

A map can tell us how big a place is, where one place is in relation to another, what a place was like in the past, and what it's like now. Maps help us understand and move through our own part of the world and the rest of the world, too. Some maps even help us move through our solar system and universe!

Terms to Know

Maps are created and designed by incorporating many different elements and accepted cartographic (mapmaking) techniques. Often, maps showing the exact same area will differ from one another, depending upon the choice or critical elements, such as scale and projection. Following is a brief listing of some key mapmaking terms.

Projection. A projection is a way to represent the round Earth on a flat surface. There are a number of different ways to project, or transfer, round-Earth information to a flat surface, though each method results in some distortion. That is, areas may appear larger or smaller than they really are—or closer or farther apart. The maps on page 6 show a few varieties of projections.

Latitude. Lines of latitude, or parallels, run parallel to the equator (the imaginary center of Earth's circumference) and are used to locate points north and south of the equator. The equator is 0 degrees latitude, the north pole is 90 degrees north latitude, and the south pole is 90 degrees south latitude.

Longitude. Lines of longitude, or meridians, run at right angles to the equator and meet at the north and south poles. Lines of longitude are used to locate points east and west of the prime meridian.

Prime meridian. An imaginary line that runs through Greenwich, England; considered 0 degrees longitude. Lines to the west of the prime meridian go halfway around the world to 180 degrees west longitude; lines to the east go to 180 degrees east longitude.

Hemisphere. A half circle. Dividing the world in half from pole to pole along the prime meridian gives you the eastern and western hemispheres. Dividing the world in half at the equator gives you the northern and southern hemispheres.

Scale. The relationship of distance on a map to the actual distance on the ground. Scale can be expressed in three ways:

    1. As a ratio—1:63,360 (one inch equals 63,360 inches)

    2. Verbally—one inch equals one mile

    3. Graphically— ☐ 1 mi.

Because 63,360 inches equal one mile, these scales give the same information: one map-inch equals one mile on the ground.

Large-scale maps show a small area, such as a city park, in great detail. Small-scale maps show a large area, such as an entire continent, in much less detail, and on a much smaller scale.

The Art and Process of Mapmaking

Maps have been made for thousands of years. Early maps, based on first-hand exploration, were some of the most accurate tools of their

◄◄ *Opposite: The maps shown here are just four of the many different projections in which the world can be displayed.*

225 million years ago

1

180 million years ago

2

65 million years ago

3

present day

4

time. Others, based on guesses about what an area was like, were often very beautiful, but were not especially accurate.

As technology—such as photography and flight—evolved, cartographers (mapmakers) were able not only to map most of Earth in detail, they were also able to make maps of our solar system.

To make a map today, cartographers first determine what a map is to show and who is most likely to use it. Then, they assemble the information they will need for the map, which can come from many different kinds of experts—such as meteorologists, geologists, and surveyors—as well as from aerial photography or satellite feedback.

Mapping a Changing Earth

If you traced around all the land masses shown on a world map, then cut them out and put them together like a jigsaw puzzle, the result would look something like map 1 at the top of this page. Scientists think this is how Earth looked about 225 million years ago.

Over time, this single continent, Pangaea (Pan–JEE–uh), slowly broke apart into two land masses called Laurasia and Gondwanaland (map 2). Maps 3 and 4 show how the land masses continued to break up and drift apart over millions of years, until the continents assumed the shapes and positions we recognize today. Earth has not, however, finished changing.

Scientists have established that Earth's surface is made up of sections called tectonic plates. These rigid plates, shown in the map on page 9, are in

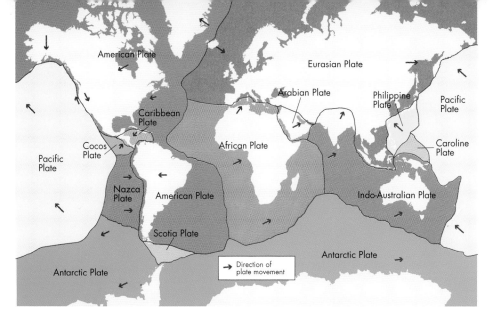

◀ **Left:** *The tectonic plates that lie beneath Earth's surface are in a slow but constant motion.*

◀◀ **Opposite:** *The continents of our planet were once clumped together but have spread apart over millions of years in what is called continental drift.*

slow, constant motion, moving from 1/4 to 1 inch a year. As they move, they take the continents and sea floors with them. Sometimes, their movements cause disasters, such as earthquakes and volcanic activity.

After many more millions of years have passed, our Earth's continents will again look very different from what we know today.

Reading a Map

In order for a map to be useful, it must be the right kind of map for the job. A small-scale map of Illinois would not help you find your way around Chicago; for that, you would need a large-scale map of the city. A physical map of North America would not tell you where most of the people live; you would need a distribution map that shows population.

Once you have found the right map, you will need to refer to the map legend, or key, to be sure you are interpreting the map's information correctly. Depending on the type of map, the legend tells the scale used for the map, and notes the meaning of any symbols and colors used.

In their most basic form, maps function as place finders. They show us where places are, and we use these maps to keep from getting lost. But as you have begun to see, maps can tell us much more about our world than simply where places are located. Just how much more, you'll discover in the chapters ahead.

Physical Map of the Atlantic Ocean Floor

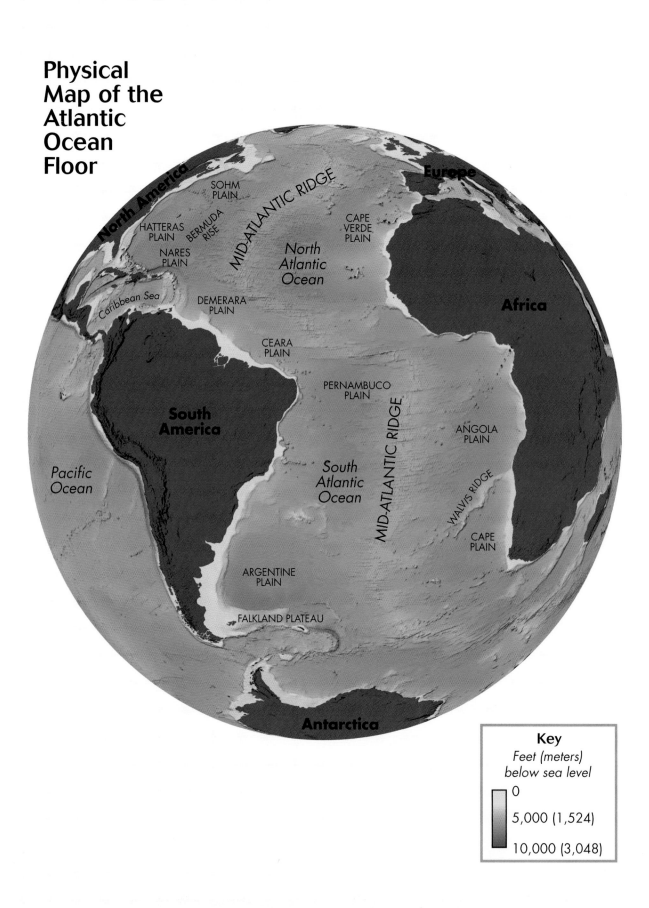

North America

Europe

SOHM PLAIN

MID-ATLANTIC RIDGE

HATTERAS PLAIN

BERMUDA RISE

CAPE VERDE PLAIN

NARES PLAIN

North Atlantic Ocean

Africa

Caribbean Sea

DEMERARA PLAIN

CEARA PLAIN

PERNAMBUCO PLAIN

South America

ANGOLA PLAIN

Pacific Ocean

South Atlantic Ocean

MID-ATLANTIC RIDGE

WALVIS RIDGE

CAPE PLAIN

ARGENTINE PLAIN

FALKLAND PLATEAU

Antarctica

Key

Feet (meters) below sea level

0

5,000 (1,524)

10,000 (3,048)

Chapter 1

Mapping the Ocean Floor

In the early days of space exploration, Earth earned the nickname "Big Blue Marble" because of the way it looks when seen from space. Earth's beautiful deep-blue color, swirled over with white clouds, is a result of the enormous amount of water on our planet. Earth is unique among the planets of our solar system in having so much water. By studying and mapping our oceans we can better understand what our world is all about.

◄ **Left:** *Oceans cover more than 70 percent of Earth.*

◄◄ **Opposite:** *The Mid-Atlantic Ridge is the longest of the ocean ridges.*

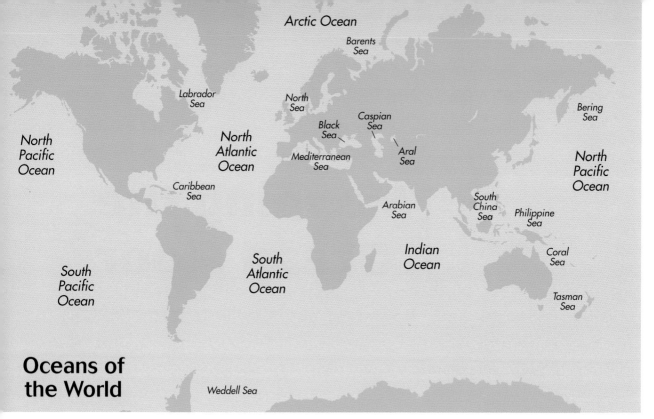

Arctic Ocean

Barents Sea

Labrador Sea

North Sea

Caspian Sea

Bering Sea

North Pacific Ocean

North Atlantic Ocean

Black Sea

Mediterranean Sea

Aral Sea

North Pacific Ocean

Caribbean Sea

Arabian Sea

South China Sea

Philippine Sea

South Pacific Ocean

South Atlantic Ocean

Indian Ocean

Coral Sea

Tasman Sea

Oceans of the World

Weddell Sea

▲ **Above:** *The Pacific and Atlantic Oceans are so large, they are divided into northern and southern sections.*

Because we are land-dwelling creatures, we tend to think of Earth in terms of land. We study the continents and their countries, learning about their physical features, the animals and plants that live there, and the history of discovery, exploration, and settlement.

But Earth's oceans cover more than 70 percent of our planet. If you look at a globe, you will see that the continents take up very little space compared to the surrounding water. To understand our world, we must understand the oceans, which are interesting and varied. Oceans contain the longest mountain range, the highest mountain, the deepest valley, and some of the most unusual animals on Earth.

Oceans are large expanses of saltwater found between continents. Smaller areas of saltwater, partly enclosed by land or near land, are called seas. Each ocean is bordered by several major seas. Although they are called seas, the Caspian and Aral seas are actually large lakes.

As the map above shows, the water covering most of Earth is divided into four oceans: the Pacific, Atlantic, Indian, and Arctic. The Pacific and Atlantic Oceans are further split by the equator into northern and southern sections. Of all the oceans, the Pacific Ocean is the largest.

The Pacific Ocean

The Pacific Ocean, as you can see from the map on page 21, is bounded on the east by North America and South America and on the west by Asia, the eastern portions of Indonesia, and Australia. It reaches from the Arctic Ocean in the north to Antarctica in the south. At its widest point, near the equator, the Pacific ocean stretches more than halfway around the world. In all, it covers more than a third of Earth's surface—just over 64 million square miles (165.8 billion square kilometers). In fact, all seven continents would fit into this ocean with enough room left over to add another one as large as Asia. The Pacific Ocean is also large enough to contain all the other oceans.

The Atlantic Ocean

The second-largest ocean is the Atlantic Ocean, with an area of almost 33 million square miles (867.7 billion square kilometers). As you can see by the map on page 10, the Atlantic Ocean is bordered by Europe and Africa on the east and by North America and South America on the west. Like the Pacific Ocean, the Atlantic reaches from the Arctic Ocean in the north to Antarctica in the South. At its widest point, the Atlantic ocean spans approximately 5,500 miles (8,800 kilometers) between North America and Europe.

The Indian Ocean

The Indian Ocean is the world's third-largest ocean. It covers an area of about 28.3 million square miles (73.3 billion square kilometers). Unlike the Pacific and Atlantic Oceans, the Indian Ocean is bordered on the north by land rather than water. Look at the map on page 14. The ocean's northern boundary is Asia, its eastern boundary is Indonesia and Australia, the western boundary is Africa, and the southern boundary is Antarctica. The widest part of the Indian Ocean is between the southern tip of Africa and Australia—about 6,200 miles (9,978 kilometers).

Physical Map of the Indian Ocean Floor

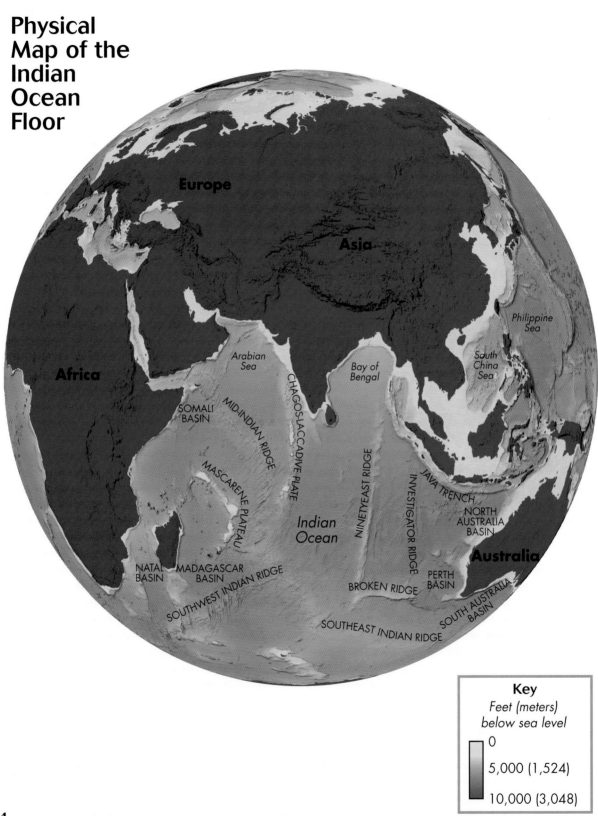

Europe

Asia

Philippine Sea

Arabian Sea

Bay of Bengal

South China Sea

Africa

SOMALI BASIN

MID-INDIAN RIDGE

CHAGOS-LACCADIVE PLATE

MASCARENE PLATEAU

Indian Ocean

NINETYEAST RIDGE

INVESTIGATOR RIDGE

JAVA TRENCH

NORTH AUSTRALIA BASIN

Australia

NATAL BASIN

MADAGASCAR BASIN

SOUTHWEST INDIAN RIDGE

BROKEN RIDGE

PERTH BASIN

SOUTH AUSTRALIA BASIN

SOUTHEAST INDIAN RIDGE

Key
Feet (meters) below sea level

0

5,000 (1,524)

10,000 (3,048)

All three of these oceans, the Pacific, Atlantic, and Indian, have very similar average depths—about 12,000 to 13,000 feet (3,658 to 3,962 meters). Ranked by average depth, the Pacific Ocean is deepest, followed by the Indian and Atlantic Oceans.

The Arctic Ocean

By far the smallest and shallowest of the world's four oceans is the Arctic Ocean. This ocean covers slightly more than 5 million square miles (13 million square kilometers) and averages about 4,000 feet (1,219 meters) deep. As you can see by the map on page 19, the ocean is bordered mostly by land. The Arctic Ocean lies at the "top" of Earth, north of Asia, Europe, and North America. The Arctic Ocean stretches from the Atlantic Ocean on the east to the Pacific Ocean on the west.

A Fifth Ocean?

Some geographers say there are five oceans, not four. They add an Antarctic Ocean to the Pacific, Atlantic, Indian, and Arctic Oceans. As you can see by turning to the map on page 16, a fifth ocean is no longer recognized.

According to the National Geographic Society, "The largest single factor in defining an ocean is the existence of a distinct basin." A basin is a huge, bowl-shaped depression that forms an ocean when it becomes filled with water. Before Antarctica was discovered, it was thought that an ocean basin lay below the south polar ice cap—the sheet of ice covering the South Pole.

Even after the discovery of Antarctica in the early 1800s, for many years it was not known whether the land beneath the ice was one of more islands. The size of the land was also in question. Once it was determined that Antarctica was a single continent nearly the size of South America, it was clear that there was no ocean basin under the South Pole. Based on this fact, most geographers agree that there is no Antarctic Ocean.

◄◄ *Opposite: The Mascarene Plateau, east of Madagascar, is a broad, flat rise.*

Physical Map of the Ocean Floor Around Antarctica

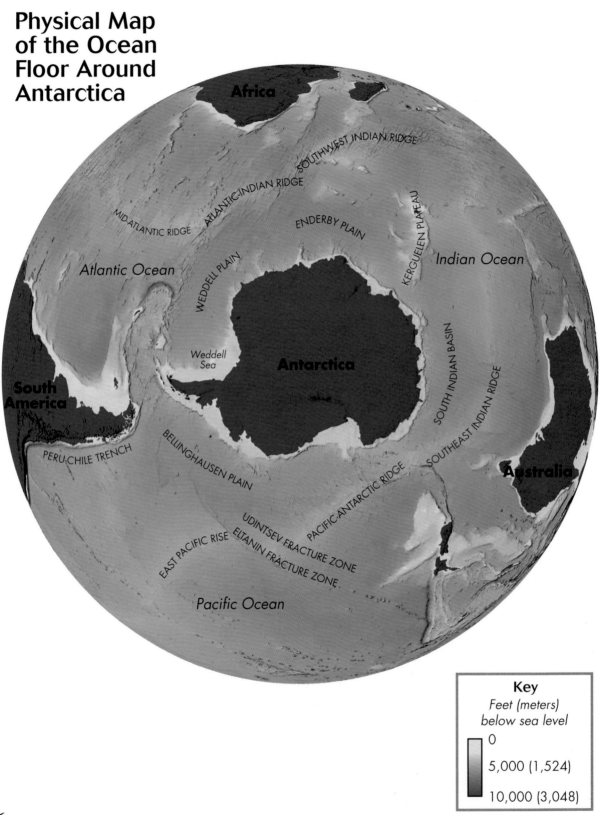

Africa

SOUTHWEST INDIAN RIDGE

ATLANTIC-INDIAN RIDGE

MID-ATLANTIC RIDGE

ENDERBY PLAIN

KERGUELEN PLATEAU

Indian Ocean

Atlantic Ocean

WEDDELL PLAIN

Weddell Sea

Antarctica

SOUTH INDIAN BASIN

SOUTHEAST INDIAN RIDGE

South America

PERU-CHILE TRENCH

BELLINGHAUSEN PLAIN

PACIFIC-ANTARCTIC RIDGE

Australia

UDINTSEV FRACTURE ZONE

EAST PACIFIC RISE

ELTANIN FRACTURE ZONE

Pacific Ocean

Key
Feet (meters) below sea level

0

5,000 (1,524)

10,000 (3,048)

The Art of Mapping Oceans

If all the water on Earth suddenly evaporated, the ocean floors would look strangely familiar to us. We would see features we already know from our study of the land, among them: towering mountains and rugged mountain chains, broad flat plains, and deep canyons. Although people have sailed the seas and oceans for thousands of years, we have only recently learned what lies beneath their surface.

A U.S. naval officer, Matthew Fontaine Maury, was the first person to make a systematic study of the ocean floor. In the early 1800s he used weighted lines to measure depths at various spots in the Atlantic Ocean and constructed contour maps from these soundings. (On a contour map, lines connect points that are at the same height or depth.) These maps and others were included in his book *The Physical Geography of the Sea*, published in 1855. Maury's findings, though very general compared to what we know today, were the first indication that the bottom of the ocean wasn't flat, as people had long supposed.

Much more information about the ocean's plant and animal life, its rocky bed, and its currents were compiled by the scientists aboard the British ship *Challenger*, which sailed the oceans for three and a half years, beginning in December 1872. The maps that were produced as a result of the expedition, however, were still based on depth measurements taken at isolated points, then strung together. They gave only a rough approximation of the ups and downs that actually lay beneath the oceans.

In the mid-1900s, echo-sounding equipment such as sonar was first used to study ocean depths. It made the scientists' work easier and more accurate. With sonar, a sound wave is sent through the water, strikes bottom, and bounces back to a receiver. The time it takes for the echo to return is recorded. By knowing how fast sound travels through water, scientists were able to tell how far away the bottom was. With sonar equipment, they could "sweep" whole sections of the ocean bottom at once and put together the first detailed topographic maps.

◄◄ *Opposite: Antarctica is bordered by three oceans.*

Although the specific topography of each ocean varies, as you can see by the physical maps on pages 10, 14, 16, 19, and 21, all of the oceans share features in common.

The Topography of the Ocean Floor

To picture the topography of an ocean, think of a bowl with a wide bottom, slanting sides, and a flat rim. The rim is the continental shelf, the sides are the continental slope, and the bottom is the ocean basin.

The Continental Shelf

The shallowest part of the oceans is the continental shelf—the area that edges the continents. On the physical maps of the oceans, these areas are light blue. A continental shelf is not completely flat but, rather, very gently sloped. The water over a continental shelf averages about 600 feet (183 meters) deep, but the width of a shelf varies considerably, as you can see on the maps.

Narrow sections—such as those along the Pacific (western) edge of North America and South America or around Africa—average about 50 miles (80.5 kilometers) wide. In some places the shelf may be as narrow as 1 mile (1.6 kilometers) wide, or it may be nonexistent. If you look along the coast of Chile on the physical map of the Atlantic Ocean (page 10), for example, you will see a stretch where the land drops abruptly into deep ocean.

In contrast, other sections of the continental shelf, such as those along northern Australia and northern Europe, (see the maps of the Pacific and Arctic Oceans on pages 21 and 19) are as much as 300 miles (483 kilometers) wide. The widest section of the continental shelf is found off northern Siberia in the Arctic Ocean. Here the shelf is nearly 1,000 miles (1,609 kilometers) wide.

The Continental Slope

The continental slope slants steeply downward from the continental shelf for about 2 miles. Underwater avalanches sweep sediment—sand

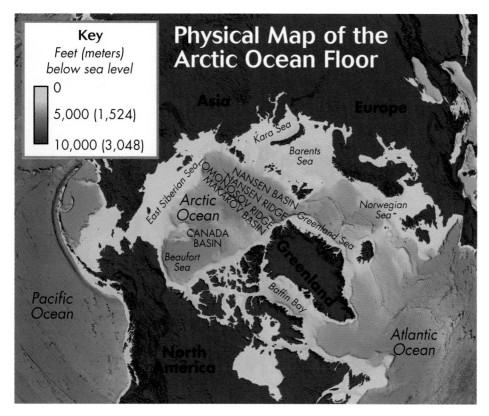

Physical Map of the Arctic Ocean Floor

Key
Feet (meters)
below sea level
0
5,000 (1,524)
10,000 (3,048)

Asia

Europe

Kara Sea

Barents Sea

East Siberian Sea

LOMONOSOV RIDGE

NANSEN RIDGE

NANSEN BASIN

MAKAROV RIDGE

Arctic Ocean

MAKAROV BASIN

Greenland Sea

Norwegian Sea

CANADA BASIN

Beaufort Sea

Greenland

Baffin Bay

Pacific Ocean

North America

Atlantic Ocean

◀ *Left:* The Arctic Ocean is smaller and shallower than the other oceans.

and mud—down from the shelf and slope. The sediment piles up at the bottom to form the continental rise, which trails off into the ocean basin—the "bottom of the bowl." Unlike a bowl, however, the bottom of the ocean is not completely flat.

Ridges

Among the most impressive features of the ocean floor are the ridges—mountain chains that are found in all the oceans. Most lie underwater. In some places, however, they rise up to form islands, such as Iceland.

The Mid-Ocean Ridge is a massive group of ridges. It winds through and connects the Pacific, Atlantic, and Indian Oceans. This interconnected mountain range is made up of the Mid-Atlantic Ridge, the East Pacific Rise, and, in the Indian Ocean, the Mideast,

Southwest, and Southeast Indian Ridges. The longest is the Mid-Atlantic Ridge, which stretches from the Arctic to Antarctica. If you look at the map of the Pacific on page 21, on the far right you will see a bit of the East Pacific Rise, which is also a mountain chain. Altogether, the chains of the Mid-Ocean Ridge measure about 40,000 (64,372 kilometers) miles long.

Seamounts

Towering underwater mountains called "seamounts" are found in all the oceans, but are most plentiful in the Pacific, as you can see by comparing the physical maps of the oceans. If you look in the north Pacific Ocean, near the center you will see one of the longest groupings of these mountains. They are known as the Emperor Seamounts. (The mountains in seamounts are more defined and less massive than a ridge.)

Plateaus and Plains

Plateaus, such as the Mascarene Plateau in the western Indian Ocean (page 14), the Kerguelen Plateau to the northeast of Antarctica (page 16), and the Falkland Plateau in the South Atlantic (page 10), are the underwater equivalents of the broad, flat rises found on land.

Contrasting with the rugged mountains and plateaus on the ocean floor are the flat areas called "abyssal plains," or simply "plains." They can be located in all four of the oceans, but they are most common in the Atlantic and least common in the Pacific. The abyssal plains are the deepest part of the ocean floor, other than the trenches.

Trenches

Ocean trenches are steep-sided, narrow valleys deep in the ocean floor. The majority of the trenches border the Pacific Ocean. If you look at the map on page 21, you will see the Mariana Trench in the western Pacific. The Mariana Trench contains the deepest point in all the oceans, the Challenger Deep. Here, the ocean floor drops nearly

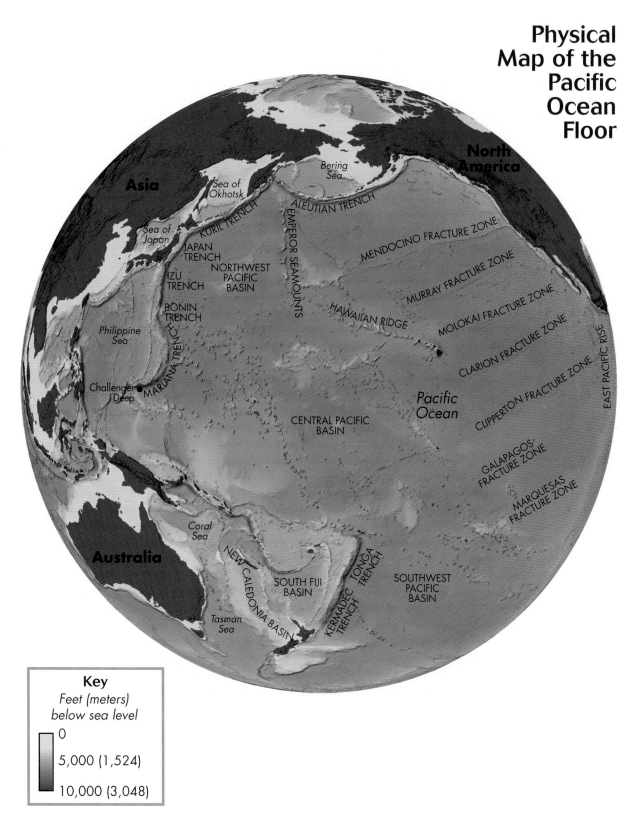

Physical Map of the Pacific Ocean Floor

Asia

North America

Bering Sea

Sea of Okhotsk

ALEUTIAN TRENCH

Sea of Japan

KURIL TRENCH

EMPEROR SEAMOUNTS

MENDOCINO FRACTURE ZONE

JAPAN TRENCH

MURRAY FRACTURE ZONE

IZU TRENCH

NORTHWEST PACIFIC BASIN

MOLOKAI FRACTURE ZONE

BONIN TRENCH

HAWAIIAN RIDGE

CLARION FRACTURE ZONE

Philippine Sea

CLIPPERTON FRACTURE ZONE

EAST PACIFIC RISE

MARIANA TRENCH

Pacific Ocean

Challenger Deep

CENTRAL PACIFIC BASIN

GALAPAGOS FRACTURE ZONE

MARQUESAS FRACTURE ZONE

Coral Sea

TONGA TRENCH

Australia

NEW CALEDONIA BASIN

SOUTH FIJI BASIN

KERMADEC TRENCH

SOUTHWEST PACIFIC BASIN

Tasman Sea

Key

Feet (meters) below sea level

0

5,000 (1,524)

10,000 (3,048)

21

▲ **Above:** *This giant clam is one of the unusual sea creatures found near sea vents.*

36,000 feet (10,973 meters) below the water's surface. That is almost 7 miles (11 kilometers)! If Mount Everest, the highest mountain on land, were dropped into the ocean at this point, you would never know the mountain was there. It would be covered by nearly 7,000 feet (2,134 meters) of water!

Temperature and Light

The temperature of the ocean water varies with its distance from the equator and with depth. Surface temperatures average 28 degrees Fahrenheit (-2 degrees Celsius) near the Arctic and Antarctic and 85 degrees Fahrenheit (29 degrees Celsius) at the equator. In general, the deeper the water, the colder it is. The water of the deep ocean floor is an average temperature of about 34 degrees Fahrenheit (7 degrees Celsius), but in the deepest trenches the water is about 28 degrees Fahrenheit (-2 degrees Celsius).

"Black Smokers"

Seawater is much hotter in the areas of thermal activity along the mid-ocean ridges. Here, at depths reaching 8,200 to 10,000 feet (2,499 to 3,048 meters), the hot water shoots up through vents (cracks) in the ridges, warming the water to as much as 500 degrees Fahrenheit (260 degrees Celsius). Minerals in the hot water form stone "chimneys" around the vents and darken the water pouring out the tops of the chimneys. This has earned the chimneys the name "black smokers." The combination of heat and minerals creates an environment that allows bacteria to grow. These bacteria in turn provide nourishment for animals such as giant 1-foot (0.3-meter)-wide clams and 10-foot (3-meter)-long tube worms that live only around the vents. Black smokers and their animal kingdoms were unknown until 1977, when they were discovered by scientists exploring undersea volcanoes in the Pacific.

Zones of Light

Sunlight, as well as temperature, determines the kind of life forms found throughout the ocean. Just as temperature varies with depth, so does light. In the clearest parts of the ocean, sunlight reaches to about 500 feet (152 meters) below the surface. The sunlit portion of the ocean is where plants grow and the most varied and abundant animal life is found.

▶ *Right:* *Sea cucumbers live in dark, deep regions of the ocean.*

Next comes the twilight zone, which extends to about 3,200 feet (975 meters) deep. Only the very smallest amount of light filters into this area, making it constantly dark and gloomy, though not pitch black. There is not enough light to support plant life, though many kinds of animals live in this zone, including squids, certain types of jellyfish and shrimp, and a variety of fish. Many of the fish, such as the lanternfish, glow in the dark.

Glow-in-the-dark fish also live in the region of total darkness below the twilight zone. An angler fish, for instance, uses a lighted "lure" that dangles from its head to attract prey. At depths of 10,000 feet (3,048 meters), sea spiders and tripod fish make their way past sea cucumbers clinging to the ocean floor. Despite their name, the "cucumbers" are not plants, but animals named for their shape. It was long thought that no life could exist much below the 10,000-foot mark. Then, in 1995, pictures taken by an unmanned submersible (an underwater craft) in the deepest part of the ocean, the Mariana Trench, showed shrimp, sea cucumbers, and jellyfish living there.

Overall, the fish of the ocean's deepest regions are a strange-looking group. They tend to be small—many are 6 inches (15 centimeters) or less in length. Their soft bodies and over-sized mouths help them survive in a world with a very limited food supply. Small bodies do not require a lot of food, and large mouths help them get what little food there is.

A Closer Look

Early scientists measured the depth of the ocean at a number of individual points, then mapped what they thought these measurements told them about the surface of the whole ocean floor. This system did not result in very accurate maps. To get an idea of the problem those scientists faced, choose a partner and turn to the physical map of the Atlantic Ocean on page 10. Draw or trace the outline of the ocean on a piece of paper and choose two colored pencils. One color will be for low spots and one for high spots.

Without looking at the map, point to a spot on the blank ocean drawing. Your partner will look at the map and say "high" or "low" depending on the depth (using the key as a guide). Mark that spot with the appropriate colored pencil. Choose a new spot and repeat the process. Do this 15 times. Now draw what you think your "soundings" tell you about the bottom. Are there a few mountains scattered around? A whole group of mountains in one area? How does your map compare with the real one?

Antarctic Gyre

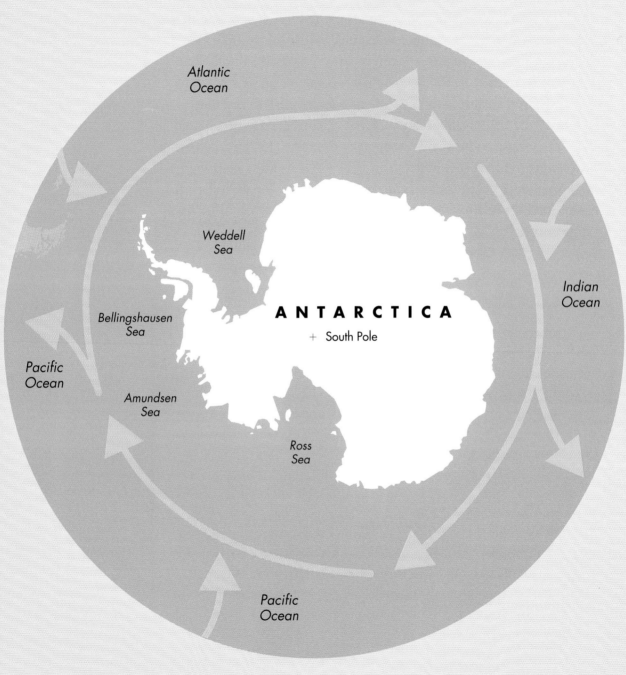

2

Exploring the Oceans

The water and land on Earth may seem to be very separate, but they are constantly interacting in ways that affect the world's weather and climate.

Wind Patterns

Wind and weather patterns are tied to the geography of the oceans. Hot air rises at the equator and flows toward the poles. As it travels, it cools and sinks back to the water's surface at around 30 degrees north latitude when heading north, and at 30 degrees south latitude when heading south. Then the air heads toward the equator again. The circulation pattern in these two bands is known as the "trade winds," and is so called because the wind pattern made it easy for sailing ships to travel across the oceans for trade.

A similar wind pattern exists between the 30- and 60-degree north and south latitudes. The winds here are called the "westerlies" because, as the map on page 28 shows, they blow from west to east. You can see that in the southern hemisphere, there is very little land to get in the way of the wind. For this reason, the southern westerlies can blow

◀ *Opposite: The Antarctic Gyre is a powerful, circular current that links the Pacific, Atlantic, and Indian Oceans.*

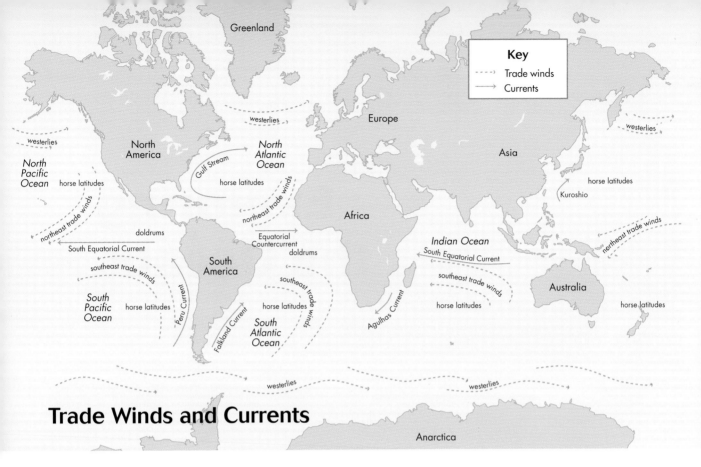

Greenland

Key
- - - Trade winds
→ Currents

Europe

Asia

westerlies

North
America

North
Atlantic
Ocean

westerlies

North
Pacific
Ocean

horse latitudes

Gulf Stream

horse latitudes

horse latitudes

Kuroshio

northeast trade winds

northeast trade winds

Africa

northeast trade winds

doldrums

South Equatorial Current

Equatorial
Countercurrent
doldrums

Indian Ocean
South Equatorial Current

southeast trade winds

South
America

southeast trade winds

southeast trade winds

Australia

South
Pacific
Ocean

horse latitudes

Peru Current

horse latitudes

Agulhas Current

horse latitudes

horse latitudes

Falkland Current

South
Atlantic
Ocean

westerlies

westerlies

Trade Winds and Currents

Anarctica

▲ **Above:** *The direction of the trade winds is influenced by the rotation of Earth.*

consistently at more than 40 miles (64 kilometers) an hour, which explains their nickname—"roaring forties."

If you look at where the equator would be on the trade winds and currents map, you will see an area marked "doldrums." Here winds blow very lightly or not at all. Sailing ships that sailed into the doldrums were often becalmed, or stalled, for weeks. A similar area of light winds lies between the trade winds and the westerlies, in both the northern and the southern hemisphere. These areas are called the "horse latitudes." The northern horse latitude was crossed by explorers sailing from Spain to the Americas. Spanish explorers took their horses with them. When their ships were becalmed, the horses eventually died from lack of food. The sailors then had to toss the animals overboard.

The winds shown on the trade winds and currents map are called "prevailing winds." These are winds that blow consistently from one direction and thus can be counted on by sailors trying to plot a course across the oceans.

Air and Water Temperature Affect Our Weather

Water heats up and cools down more slowly than land. This means that in winter, the water is warmer than the land, and in summer, it is cooler. As a result, coastal areas generally have cooler summers and warmer winters than inland regions.

Air temperature also affects precipitation. The warmer the air, the more moisture it can hold. The warmest, wettest air is found along the equator over the oceans. As this air moves over nearby land, the moisture is lost as rain, making coastal regions near the equator among the wettest places on Earth. Coastal areas in general tend to be wetter than inland areas because air coming off the ocean loses moisture as it travels inland. This pattern is not consistent, however. The Atacama Desert, one of the driest places on Earth, is on Chile's northern coast.

Hurricanes and Tsunamis

Hurricanes are immense circular storms that begin over the ocean. They are generated by warm, moist air that is drawn upward in a spiral pattern. Hurricanes arise in the warmer parts of the oceans, where the trade winds blow. Once a hurricane moves over colder water or over land, it gradually loses power.

Tsunamis are destructive waves caused by underwater earthquakes or volcanic eruptions. Although a tsunami travels at more than 400 miles (644 kilometers) per hour, in the open ocean, it hardly ruffles the water's surface. If it reaches land, however, it slows down and rises up as much as 100 feet (30 meters) before crashing on the coast.

A tsunami does not have to be that high to cause extensive damage and much loss of life, however. On July 17, 1998, an earthquake occurred about 12 miles (19 kilometers) off the north coast of Papua New Guinea, an island country just north of Australia. A 23-foot (7-meter) tsunami, about the height of a three-story building, smashed onto the coast, wiping out three villages and killing thousands of people. Because the earthquake occurred so close to shore, there was no time for people to flee inland before the tsunami hit. By the time they felt the tremor of the quake, the wave had already reached land.

The ocean's heating, cooling, and precipitation effects on land would occur even if the ocean stood still. The moving air would see to that. However, the ocean does not stand still. And, its movement also affects weather and climate.

Ocean Currents

Currents are bands of water that flow through the world's oceans like rivers. Surface currents are caused by the wind, which sweeps the water along. Although they are called "surface currents," they are generally from 300 to 600 feet (91 to 183 meters) deep.

In the open ocean, major currents connect and flow in huge, circular patterns called "gyres." Look again at the winds and currents map on page 28. The northeast and southeast trade winds drive five gyres: two in the Atlantic Ocean, two in the Pacific Ocean, and one in the Indian Ocean. If you follow the general path of the trade winds, you will see that they tend to bend to the right north of the equator and to the left south of the equator. This is caused by the rotation of Earth. It is called the Coriolis Effect, after the French mathematician Gaspard de Coriolis, who first described it. The Coriolis Effect and the influence of the continents edging the oceans cause gyres in the northern hemisphere to flow clockwise and gyres in the southern hemisphere to flow counterclockwise.

The Antarctic gyre, shown on the map on page 26, is driven by the winds of the southern westerlies. This gyre is composed of only one current, the Antarctic Circumpolar Current. It is the largest and strongest of the currents and the only one that directly links all the oceans, except for the Arctic.

Ocean Currents and Weather

Just as winds distribute warm and cold air around Earth, ocean currents distribute warm and cold water. For example, the Gulf Stream, which is the second-largest current in the oceans, carries warm water from the Gulf of Mexico northeast to the British Isles and to the west coast of Norway. The moderating effect of the Gulf Stream gives those areas a milder climate than other places located at the same distance from the equator.

The Gulf Stream

One of the best-known currents, the Gulf Stream, was first mapped by Benjamin Franklin in the 1750s, while he was deputy postmaster general for the American colonies. He hoped that ships carrying mail from England would use his map to avoid sailing against the current and get the mail to America faster!

Benjamin Franklin

The Peru Current and "El Niño"

A current shift, or a change in a current, can seriously affect weather patterns. One of the best-known examples of this is the weather that accompanies the current shift known as El Niño ("The Child"). It is so named because it usually occurs around Christmas time.

Normally, a cold current flows northward along the coast of South America up to Peru. This Peru Current was originally called the Humboldt Current after the German scientist and explorer Alexander von Humboldt. From 1799 to 1804, Humboldt did extensive natural research in Mexico, Central America, and South America on everything from plants to ocean currents. He was the first person to make a map using isotherms—lines connecting points having the same temperature.

About every six years, the cold Peru Current is replaced by El Niño, a warm current that disrupts weather patterns worldwide. Areas that are normally dry experience torrential rains. Other areas suffer through months-long droughts. Eventually, the current pattern returns to normal, and so does the world's weather, but often not before a great deal of natural and economic damage has been done.

Pacific Trade Routes

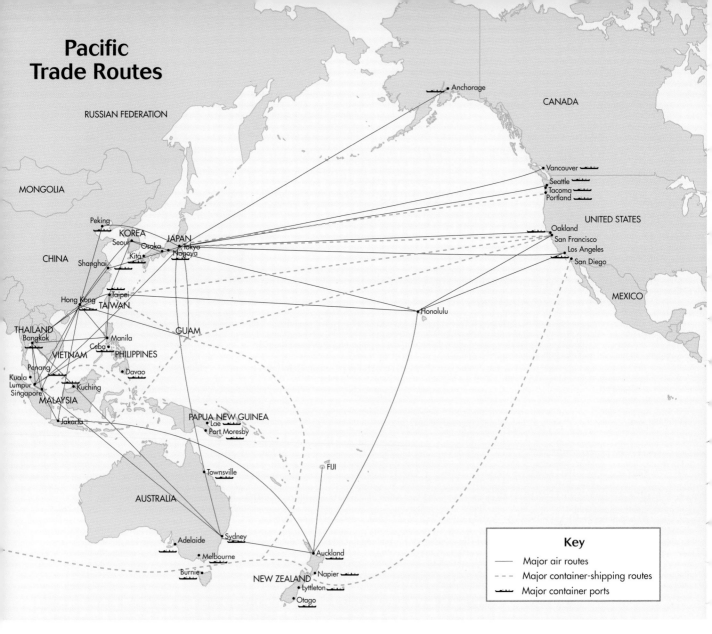

Key

— Major air routes

--- Major container-shipping routes

⊸⊸⊸ Major container ports

▲ *Above: Many of the port cities on the West Coast of the United States receive container ships.*

The Ocean "Highway"

The oceans and seas have been used as a "highway" for thousands of years. The earliest and most basic method of transportation was a simple log boat, canoe, or raft powered by hand or with paddles. It was not until about 3000 B.C., when Egyptians invented sails, that the power of the wind could be used to speed up a journey and take boats farther. Early ocean travelers, such as the Polynesians who sailed the South Pacific around 2000 B.C., depended heavily on their knowledge of winds and currents to make their trips easier and faster.

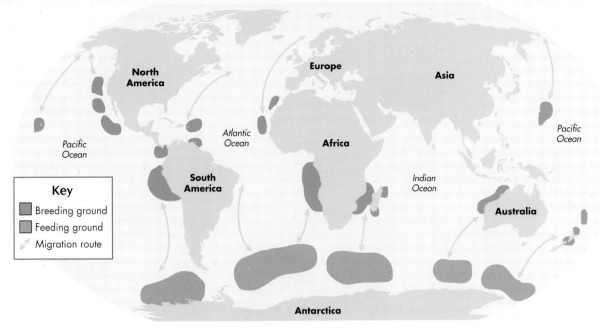

Humpback Whale Migration

Once engines and propellers came into use in the mid-1800s, ships became faster still and less dependent on winds and currents. This meant that goods could be moved more easily via the ocean than ever before. Today, the majority of the world's cargo is carried by container ships, which carry cargo in large, metal containers.

The Atlantic is the world's busiest ocean, but the Pacific also sees a lot of trade, as the map of Pacific trade routes on page 32 shows. Many of the major cities that border the Pacific are ports for container ships, including 11 ports in the South Pacific. Japan and Hong Kong are hubs for air traffic in the Pacific.

Ships are not the only ocean travelers that follow special routes. Whales regularly migrate between their breeding grounds, located in warmer waters, and their feeding grounds, which are in colder waters, where their food is more plentiful. As you can see by the map above, the primary feeding grounds for humpback whales in the southern hemisphere are located off Antarctica.

▲ *Above: The largest breeding grounds for humpback whales are off the coasts of South America and Africa.*

▼ *Below: A humpback whale breaches, or breaks through, the water.*

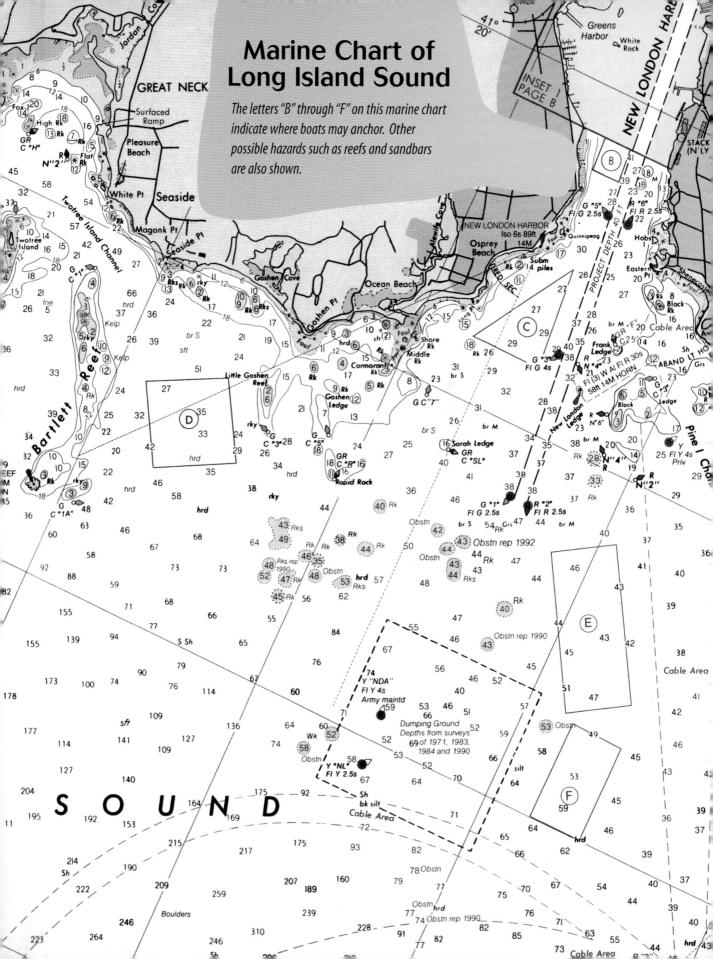

Marine Chart of Long Island Sound

The letters "B" through "F" on this marine chart indicate where boats may anchor. Other possible hazards such as reefs and sandbars are also shown.

Marine Charts

Safe navigation, whether for trade or pleasure, depends on a good knowledge of the ocean floor, particularly when a boat nears shore. There, such things as reefs, sandbars, or sunken debris can cause sudden changes in the water depth, which pose danger to a boat or ship. Detailed marine charts (maps) such as the one on the opposite page, are used to guide boats safely through the water. The numbers represent various depths, and individual obstructions, such as Bartlett Reef, are labeled. In the dumping ground area (lower right), it tells what year the depths were surveyed. This serves as a warning that the depths may not be exactly as represented on the map. The areas marked B through F are general anchorage areas.

◀ *Left:* Ships, such as this cruiser, must consult marine charts carefully to help them navigate around dangerous underwater terrain.

What the Oceans Hold for the Future

The oceans will undoubtedly be used as highways for trade and recreation as far into the future as we can imagine. And if we are careful about conservation, the oceans will continue to be sources of food. Although the oceans' energy resources—oil and gas—cannot be renewed, further exploration and mapping is expected to uncover new oil and gas fields. Some of them may lie much deeper than the ones currently under production, and will require the invention of new drilling techniques to be accessed.

Special mining techniques will also be needed to make the mining of manganese nodules a commercial success. As exploration has shown, billions of tons of these mineral-rich, potato-shaped lumps lie on the ocean floor. (Manganese is used to harden steel.) While some nodule mining has been done already, it is currently an expensive effort that isn't practical on a large scale.

In the future, tides and waves may be routinely harnessed to provide a new source for electric power. Presently, there is a tidal power station across the mouth of France's Rance River, where it empties into the Atlantic Ocean.

◀◀ *Opposite: While harvesting the natural resources of the sea, we must protect the delicate balance of the underwater ecosystems.*

A Closer Look

In the days of sailing ships, navigators depended on their knowledge of wind and current patterns to make their voyages as easy and quick as possible. Look at the trade winds map on page 28. Keeping the winds in mind, which route would you rather sail, and why?

Would you travel from Spain to Greenland or Spain to Brazil? Would you travel from western Australia to South Africa or southern Brazil to northwest Africa?

Constellations in the Northern Sky

3

Exploring the Skies and Universe

If you are lucky, one day you might get a chance to see the bottom of Challenger Deep, the deepest spot in the oceans, at nearly 7 miles (11 kilometers) below the water's surface. But right now, if you look up instead of down, you can see much farther than that! You can see objects that are millions upon millions of miles beyond the surface of Earth.

What You Can See in the Sky

By looking at the sky at night without binoculars or a telescope, it's possible to see a moon, stars, planets, comets, meteors, and, depending on where you are, a galaxy or two. A galaxy is a huge grouping of billions of stars, dust, and gas.

Stars

During the day, the only star you can see is the one nearest to Earth—the sun. At night, however, if you are outside of a city and the moon is not too full, you can see between 2,000 and 3,000 stars. Although this is a great many, it is only a small fraction of all the stars in the universe. Most of the stars that you can see belong to our

◀◀ *Opposite:* The North Star is the northernmost star of Ursa Minor, at the center of the map.

galaxy, the Milky Way. But there are many more stars in the Milky Way that you can't see. Our galaxy contains hundreds of billions of stars. And there are more than 50 billion galaxies in the universe!

People have studied and mapped the sky since ancient times, using the information to establish calendars, plant their crops, and navigate their ships. They saw patterns in certain groups of bright stars that reminded them of people, animals, and objects. These constellations were elaborately reproduced on early sky charts, not just with stars, but also with beautiful pictures. As European explorers sailed into the southern oceans, they discovered new stars and named new constellations.

Perhaps the most important constellation in the northern hemisphere is *Ursa Minor*, which is Latin for "Small Bear." You will find it at the center of the constellations chart of the northern sky on page 38. Its position never changes. The major stars of this constellation form a pattern that we call the Little Dipper. The brightest star in this grouping is Polaris, found at the end of the dipper's handle. Polaris is also called the North Star because it's located directly over the North Pole. In the days before navigational tools were invented, sailors used the North Star to keep their boats on course. That's because Polaris never changes position—even as the rest of the stars in the constellation and all of the other constellations appear to move through the sky. Actually, it is Earth that is moving; rotating on its axis and orbiting the sun. Because of Earth's movements, we face different sections of the sky at different times of the day and in different seasons. This gives us the different views of the sky and its constellations.

There is no star directly over the South Pole in the southern hemisphere, but Crux, also called Southern Cross, can be used to find the approximate location of the South Pole. You'll find Crux below and to the right of center on the constellations map of the southern sky on the opposite page.

Over time, constellations were created to include fainter stars and fill in the spaces between the major star groups. Some constellations

▶▶ *Opposite: The constellations that are visible from the southern skies (shown here) and from the northern skies are all in the Milky Way.*

Constellations in the
Southern Sky

were sub-divided into several constellations. For example, there was a large constellation in the southern hemisphere called Argo ("the ship") that was split into three parts: Carina ("the keel"), Puppis ("the deck"), and Vela ("the sails"). If you look northeast of the center of the constellations map (page 41) you will find these constellations.

There are 88 constellations recognized by astronomers around the world. The squared-off boundaries of the constellations, when they are marked on a map, divide up the entire sky much like the way boundaries of countries divide up a continent. Everything in space falls within the boundaries of one constellation or another. However, astronomers use much more precise measurements than the name of a constellation to refer to an object's location.

Planets

In addition to stars, you can see several planets with the naked eye. Venus, Mars, and Jupiter are the brightest and easiest to spot. Mercury can only be seen just after sunset or before sunrise, when it is briefly distinguishable from the sun's glare. Saturn is so faint it looks like a star. However, planets do not make their own light, the way stars do. Planets shine because they reflect sunlight.

▶ *Right:* *An artist's picture of the space probe* Galileo *approaching Jupiter in 1995.*

42

Moons, Comets, and Meteors

Moons, natural satellites that orbit planets, also shine by reflecting sunlight. Earth's moon is close, about 239,000 miles (384,623 kilometers) away. Our moon is a familiar object in the night sky, but the moons of the other planets are too far away and faint for you to see without the aid of binoculars or a telescope.

Comets are lumps of dust and ice that orbit the sun, usually at a great distance from Earth. We can see one when its orbit brings it close to Earth. Space dirt and rocks that fall into Earth's atmosphere burn up as meteors. Though meteors are often called shooting stars, they are not stars at all.

Measuring the Distances

The vast distances of stellar (star) space are measured in light years. This is the distance light travels in one year, almost 6 trillion miles!

▲ *Above:* The large Magellanic Cloud (top left) and the small Magellanic cloud (bottom right) are small galaxies in orbit around our own galaxy— the Milky Way.

The most distant object that can be seen in space with the naked eye is the Andromeda galaxy. It lies more than 2 million light years away in the northern constellation Andromeda (refer to the map on page 38). Two closer galaxies, the Large Magellanic Cloud (170,000 light years away) and the Small Magellanic Cloud (190,000 light years away), can be seen from the Southern Hemisphere (see the map on page 41). These galaxies were named for Ferdinand Magellan, the great Portuguese navigator of the early 1500s.

Technology for Viewing the Details

The invention of the telescope in 1608, by the Dutch eyeglass maker Hans Lippershey, began a new era in astronomy. Astronomers could finally see in detail the stars and other objects they had been tracking for centuries. Telescopes also offered the opportunity to probe farther into space.

In 1609, the Italian scientist Galileo built his own, improved, telescopes with which he made a number of findings. Galileo discovered sun spots, the phases of Venus, and the four largest of Jupiter's moons. Galileo also realized that the "shadows" on the surface of the moon were actually craters and mountains. His detailed sketches of the moon were the first maps of a heavenly body other than Earth. By the mid-1600s, the first lunar atlas was published by the Polish astronomer Johannes Hevelius, who mapped more than 250 of the moon's features.

A simplified, modern map of one section of the moon is shown on the opposite page. The smaller features are craters and the large features are broad plains. Because early astronomers mistook the moon's plains for seas, they named them that way. *Mare Tranquillitatis*, for example, means the "Sea of Tranquility" in Latin. In 1969, nearly 300 years after Hevelius produced his atlas, the U.S. spaceship *Apollo 11* made the first manned moon landing on the Sea of Tranquility.

In addition to the continuing refinement of the telescope, the invention of photography in the 1830s helped mapmakers to create

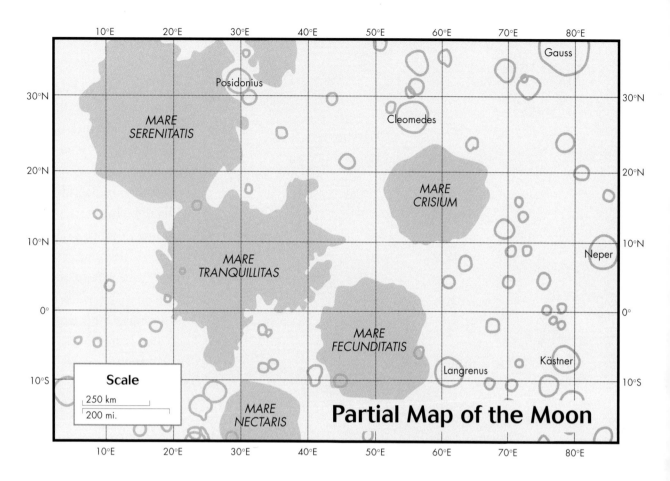

Partial Map of the Moon

Scale

250 km

200 mi.

MARE SERENITATIS

Posidonius

MARE TRANQUILLITAS

MARE NECTARIS

MARE FECUNDITATIS

MARE CRISIUM

Gauss

Cleomedes

Neper

Langrenus

Kästner

more detailed maps of the skies. In the twentieth century, satellites, space probes, and planetary landers revealed much more information about the universe. Satellites, carrying cameras and orbiting Earth above the atmosphere, allowed the first truly clear pictures of space to be taken. Unmanned spacecraft, sent into orbit to explore the universe, collect information about the planets of our solar system, as seen close up, from space. Planetary landers send back even more detailed pictures. They can also perform maneuvers, such as scooping up soil samples, which provide information about the surface and composition of the planets.

Although the surface of Mars was first observed in 1659 through a telescope, astronomers of that time couldn't begin to imagine the details that the space probe *Pathfinder* beamed back to Earth in 1997. Detailed photographs enable astronomers to construct topographical maps such as the one on page 46. In this view of Mars, you will find

▲ *Above:* The large deep blue regions on this map of the moon are plains.

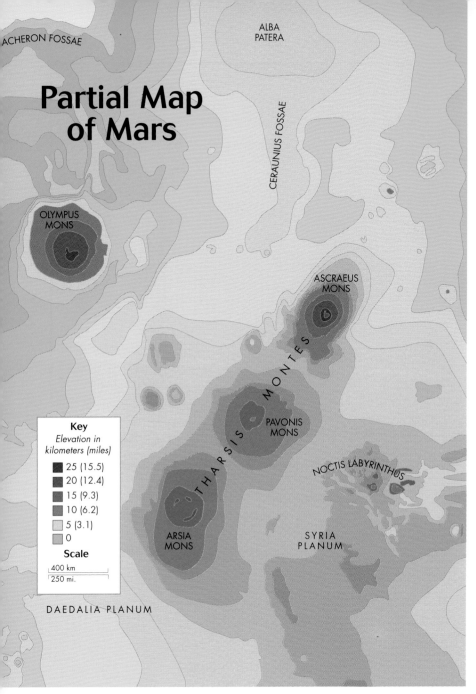

Partial Map of Mars

ACHERON FOSSAE

ALBA PATERA

CERAUNIUS FOSSAE

OLYMPUS MONS

ASCRAEUS MONS

THARSIS MONTES

PAVONIS MONS

NOCTIS LABYRINTHUS

ARSIA MONS

SYRIA PLANUM

Key

Elevation in kilometers (miles)

- 25 (15.5)
- 20 (12.4)
- 15 (9.3)
- 10 (6.2)
- 5 (3.1)
- 0

Scale

400 km
250 mi.

DAEDALIA PLANUM

▲ *Above: Olympus Mons, in the western part of this map of Mars, is probably the tallest volcano in the solar system.*

several volcanoes (labeled "mons" or "patera"), two upland plains ("planum"), two grooved areas ("fossae"), and a ridge (Tharsis Montes). The volcano Olympus Mons is one of the planet's most famous features. At more than 15 miles (25 kilometers) high, this volcano is nearly three times the height of Mt. Everest and is believed to be the tallest volcano in the solar system.

The Solar System and Beyond

Most early astronomers thought that Earth was the center of the universe, and everything revolved around our planet. In A.D. 150, the astronomer and geographer Ptolemy published *The Almagest*, a book that catalogued more than 1,000 stars and presented a detailed structure of an unchanging Earth-centered sky.

In 1543, the Polish astronomer Copernicus claimed that Earth revolved around the sun, rather than vice versa. His theory stimulated an ongoing debate and study of the universe that lasted for another 50 years. Galileo's discovery of the phases of Venus finally proved that

Copernicus was correct. His discovery showed that Venus orbited the sun, and not Earth. The mapping of the universe, as we know it today, began to take shape. You can get an idea of the immense size of the universe, and our relative place in it, by examining the maps that follow.

Mapping the Universe

As you study the following maps, you will see that many of them look quite different from the ones you are used to using. This is because objects in space do not lie on a flat surface. They lie at all different levels and directions from each other—like fish floating in an aquarium. Trying to show these relationships is what makes the neighboring stars, local group, and local supercluster maps on pages 49–55 look so different. However, the maps still contain familiar elements such as titles, keys, and distance scales. On these maps, the vast distances in the universe are measured in light years. Each circular band marks the number of light years from the central position on each map.

For practice using these maps, look at the neighboring stars map on page 49. The center of the mapped area is our sun, and the bands mark distances from the sun in 5-light-year units. Now, locate the star Alpha Centauri, then follow the dotted line down to the distance scale. You can see that this star lies lower in space than the sun and not quite 5 light years away. Giclas 51-15, on the other hand, lies higher in space and about 10 light years away.

The Solar System

Until the late 1700s, only six of the planets, Mercury through Saturn, were shown on maps of the solar system. Then in 1781, Uranus was discovered. Shortly after, Neptune was sited and added to the map of the solar system in 1846. Pluto was first seen less than 100 years ago, in 1930.

Space probes have enabled scientists to discover what the planets are made of and to categorize them accordingly. The inner planets,

Inner Solar System

Mercury · Sun · Venus · Earth · Mars · Asteroid belt

▲ **Above:** *The inner solar system is surrounded by a belt of thousands of asteroids.*

▼ **Below:** *Although Pluto is usually the planet that is farthest from the sun, sometimes Neptune's orbit takes it farther away.*

shown on the map above, are rocky. The mostly giant planets of the outer solar system (below)—Jupiter, Saturn, Uranus, and Neptune—are largely liquid and gas. Pluto, the smallest and farthest planet that we now know of in our solar system, is thought to have a frozen gas surface. Except for Pluto, all of the outer planets have rings, which are composed of dust, rocks, or ice. The asteroid belt that orbits the sun between Mars and Jupiter was added to maps of the solar system after its discovery at the beginning of the 1800s.

As its name implies, the belt is made up of asteroids, large pieces of rocky debris left over from the time the solar system formed.

Outer Solar System

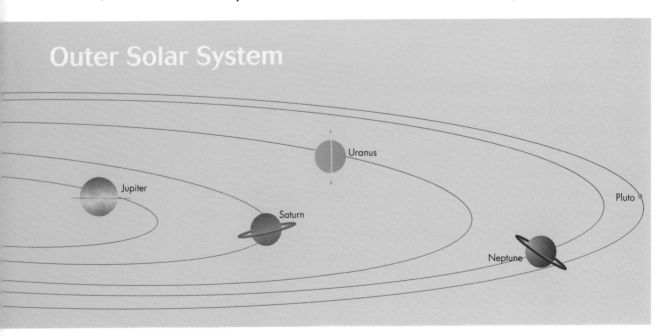

Jupiter · Saturn · Uranus · Neptune · Pluto

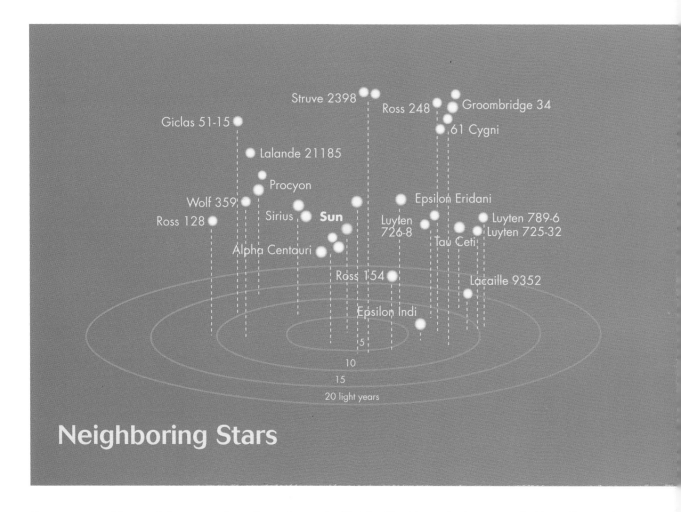

Giclas 51-15

Struve 2398

Ross 248   Groombridge 34

61 Cygni

Lalande 21185

Procyon

Wolf 359

Ross 128

Sirius   **Sun**

Epsilon Eridani

Luyten
726-8

Luyten 789-6
Luyten 725-32

Tau Ceti

Alpha Centauri

Ross 154

Lacaille 9352

Epsilon Indi

5
10
15
20 light years

Neighboring Stars

Some asteroids are big enough to have been individually identified and given names. Ceres is the largest, with a diameter of about 600 miles. Most of the thousands of asteroids in the belt are much smaller.

Neighboring Stars

When you look at a constellation, the stars appear to be close together and the same distance from Earth. However, the map above shows that stars that appear near each other are actually light years apart in space. Measuring the distances to the nearest stars, to the sun, and to Earth gave astronomers a way of mapping the entire universe.

▲ *Above: The stars shown on this map that are farthest from the sun are a little more than 10 light years away from it.*

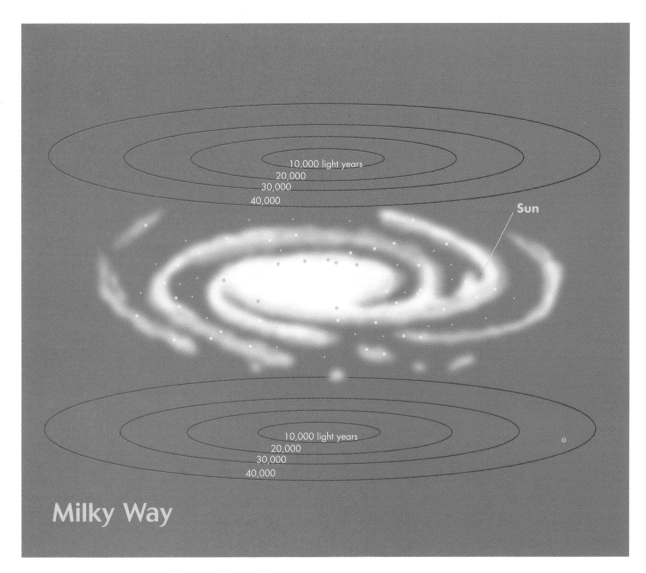

10,000 light years
20,000
30,000
40,000

Sun

10,000 light years
20,000
30,000
40,000

o

Milky Way

▲ *Above: The reddish stars near the middle of the Milky Way are the oldest stars in the galaxy.*

The Milky Way

Our solar system, all of the neighboring stars, and hundreds of billions more are part of the Milky Way Galaxy. If you look at the map of the Milky Way above, you will see that our sun, and therefore our solar system, is located toward the edge of the galaxy. Although some galaxies exist by themselves in space, most belong to clusters that include other galaxies.

Local Group

Astronomers once thought that the Milky Way was the only galaxy. In fact, they thought that the Milky Way was the entire universe. In 1929, however, the American astronomer Edwin Hubble determined that this was not true. With his powerful telescope he discovered there were other galaxies besides ours.

We now map our galaxy as part of a cluster known as Local Group (shown below). There are about 30 other galaxies in Local Group. As you have seen, the Milky Way is huge, but it is only the second-largest galaxy in this cluster. The Andromeda Galaxy, above and to the left of the Milky Way, is the largest. It's about twice as big as the Milky Way.

▼ *Below:* Local Group is a cluster of about 30 galaxies.

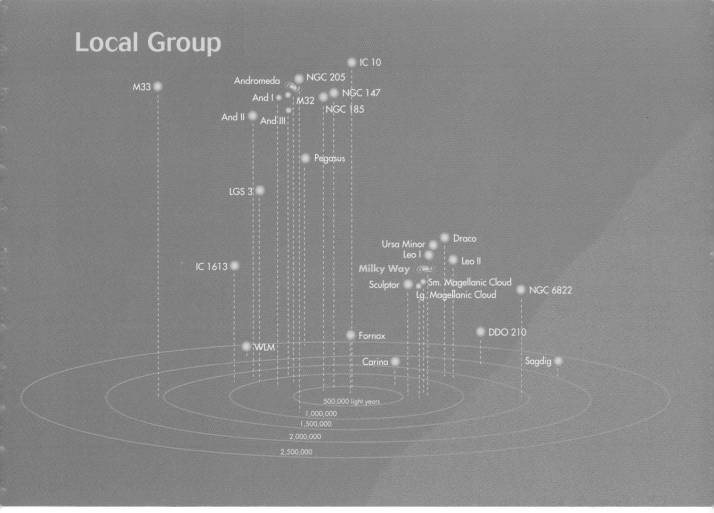

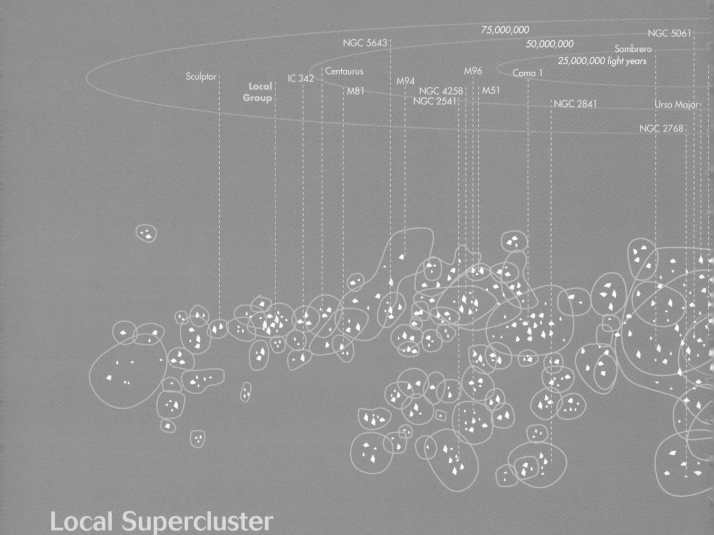

75,000,000

NGC 5643

50,000,000

NGC 5061

Sombrero

25,000,000 *light years*

Sculptor

Centaurus

M96

Coma 1

Local Group

IC 342

M94

M81

NGC 4258

M51

NGC 2541

NGC 2841

Ursa Major

NGC 2768

Local Supercluster

Local Supercluster

▲ *Above: The Virgo Cluster, at the center of this Supercluster, contains about 200 galaxies.*

Local Supercluster

Our Local Group is in turn a member of the Local Supercluster (shown above), which is made up of over 100 galaxy clusters. You can find Local Group off to the left side of the Local Supercluster. As you can see from this map, galaxy clusters come in many sizes. Our Local Group, with 30 galaxies, is relatively small. In contrast, the Virgo cluster, in the middle of the map, contains about 200 bright galaxies. And, as you can see, even that cluster is not the biggest.

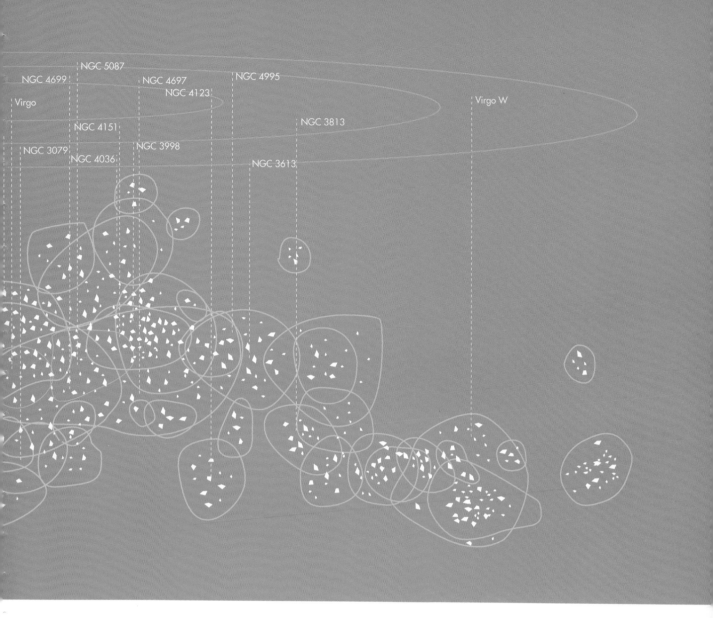

NGC 5087
NGC 4699
NGC 4697
NGC 4995
Virgo
NGC 4123
NGC 4151
NGC 3813
Virgo W
NGC 3079
NGC 3998
NGC 4036
NGC 3613

The Known Universe

Finally, look at the map on page 54. You can barely make out the Local Supercluster, and the Sun, so important in our day-to-day lives, is smaller than a speck of dust. In fact, because these maps are so incredibly small scale, and cover such vast distances, the sun is unidentifiable on any maps that include more of the universe than the Milky Way.

The Known Universe

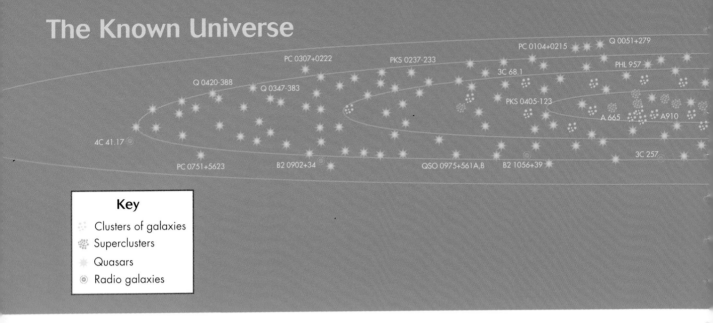

Key

* Clusters of galaxies
* Superclusters
* Quasars
* Radio galaxies

Map labels: PC 0104+0215, Q 0051+279, PHL 957, PC 0307+0222, PKS 0237-233, 3C 68.1, Q 0420-388, Q 0347-383, PKS 0405-123, A 665, A910, 4C 41.17, PC 0751+5623, B2 0902+34, QSO 0975+561A,B, B2 1056+39, 3C 257

▲ *Above: Although the outer boundary of the universe is shown to be 20 billion light years from the center, astronomers don't really know how big the universe is. And it's still expanding!*

Gravity Keeps It All Together

Since the 1600s, when Sir Isaac Newton discovered gravity, the notion that matter can exert force on other matter has reshaped how we map the universe. Once Newton described how gravity worked to keep the planets in orbit around the sun, and the moon in orbit around the Earth, astronomers realized that the same idea could be extened to the rest of the universe.

The gravitational force exerted by the sun keeps the nine planets in our solar system from flying out into deep space. In the same way, the pull exerted by the center of our galaxy prevents its stars from being thrown into the intergalactic void. Since galaxies themselves are so massive, the gravity they generate pulls other galaxies into local groups, like the one we share with the Andromeda Galaxy and the Large and Small Magellanic Clouds. Local groups, in turn, pull into superclusters. Gravity gives shape to the universe.

The Big Bang

Look again at the known universe map. You will see that the most distant objects lie between 15 and 20 billion light years from the center of the map, where our supercluster is located. However, even though the outer edge of the universe is shown as 20 billion light

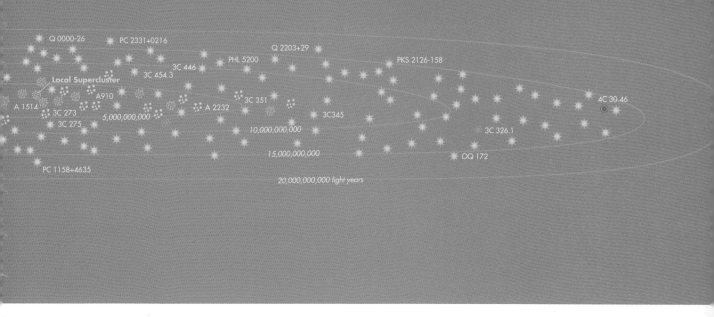

years away, there is really no set limit to its size. This is because the universe has been expanding since it was first formed.

When Edwin Hubble proved in 1929 that our galaxy was not the only galaxy in space, he also showed that the galaxies were moving outward. This discovery led scientists to develop a "Big Bang" theory. According to this theory, which is accepted by most astronomers, the universe began with an explosion of energy. This explosion resulted in a massive, swirling, cloud of particles that eventually, over thousands of years, clumped together to form galaxies. But even then, the force of the explosion continued to push these galaxies outward.

It might help to understand this theory if you picture a very small balloon filled with tiny bits of sticky confetti. If you blow up the balloon quickly to the point where it explodes, the confetti will fly outward. And if you take a slow-motion picture of this burst, you will be able to see that the bits of confetti stick together in various clumps, like galaxies. These clumps continue to spread outward for a long time. This is the point at which the universe is now.

Scientists do not know if the universe will continue expanding forever or if it will eventually, after trillions of years, slow down and then begin to contract—like a stretched rubberband snapping back, only more slowly.

Pulsars, Quasars, and Black Holes in the Northern Sky

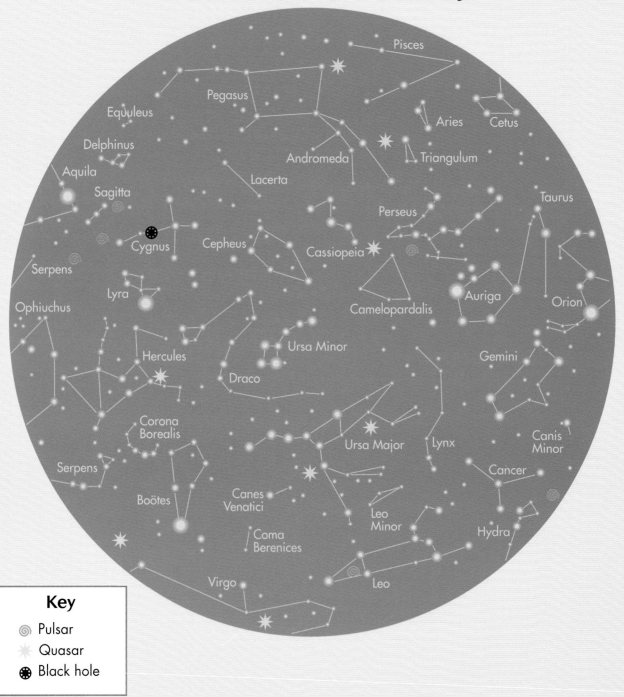

Pulsars, Quasars, and Black Holes

Just as the depths of the oceans became even more mysterious as they were first explored, so it was with space. Newer telescopes and photographic techniques turned up odd occurrences such as pulsars, quasars, and black holes.

Stars, including our sun, don't live forever. Eventually they die. Toward the end of their lives they swell up many times their size and become red giants. At this point they may collapse slowly or explode in a burst called a "supernova." If a star collapses slowly, its core forms a hot white dwarf, then gradually burns out. If a star explodes in a supernova, its core becomes a dense neutron star. These neutron

◄◄ *Opposite:*
Astronomers believe that in the northern sky, there is a black hole in the constellation Cygnus.

▼ *Below: The Vela supernova remnant (remains) is about 1,500 light years from Earth.*

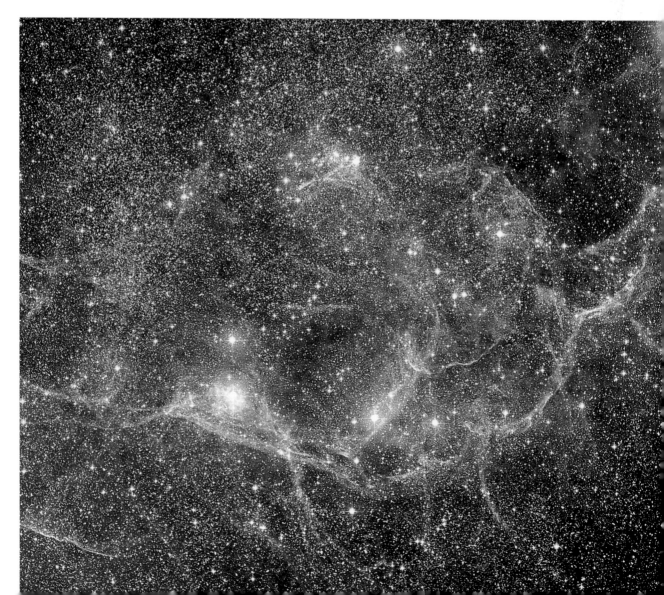

Pulsars, Quasars, and Black Holes in the Southern Sky

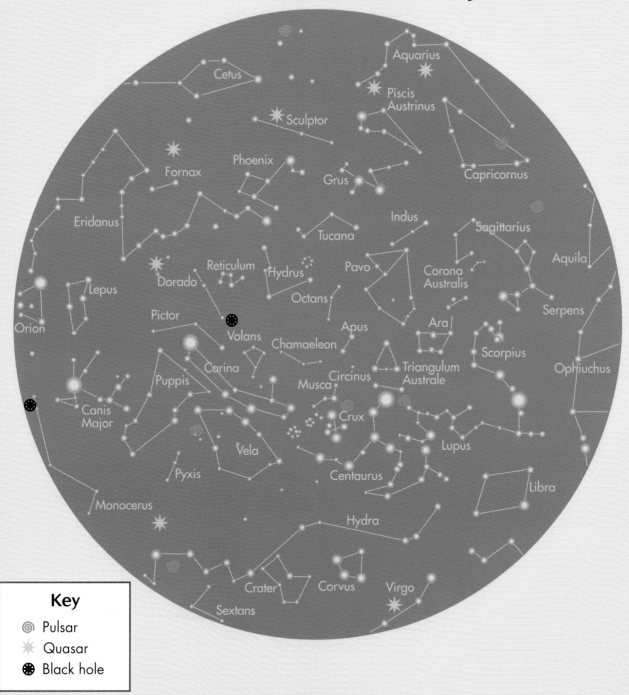

Key

◎ Pulsar

✴ Quasar

⬤ Black hole

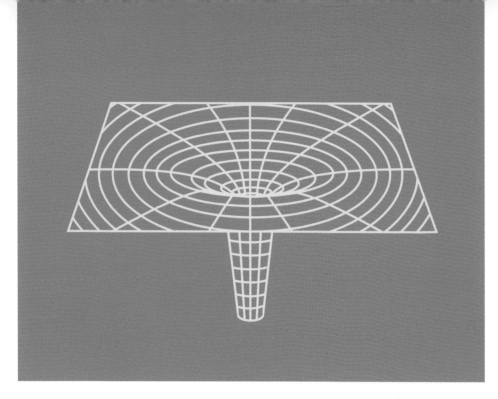

Left: Nothing can escape the gravity force of a black hole.

Opposite: Although only a handful of quasars have been found in the southern sky, thousands have been found outside of our galaxy.

stars spin very quickly, at up to 30 turns a second. With each spin, they give off a flash of energy. At this stage, they are pulsars.

Sometimes a burned-out star's core shrinks to about 37 miles (60 kilometers) in diameter, becoming so dense that it collapses on itself and becomes a black hole. Though real, a black hole is the stuff of science fiction. Its gravity is so strong that it pulls everything nearby into the hole. Nothing can escape the force, not even light. Scientists are able to "see" black holes by locating regions where gas and light are disappearing into nothingness.

A quasar is a star-like object about the size of our solar system, but with the mass (amount of material) of an entire galaxy. An enormous black hole lies at the quasar's center, but the quasar's mass is too dense to just slip through the hole. Instead, everything swirls and rumbles around the center. As a result of this commotion, a quasar gives off huge amounts of energy in the form of light and radio waves. Thousands of quasars have been found since they were first identified in the early 1960s. Most of them are at the center of young galaxies in the outer reaches of the universe, as the map on pages 54–55 indicates. This is also the location of radio galaxies—distant galaxies that emit powerful radio waves. Radio waves are electromagnetic

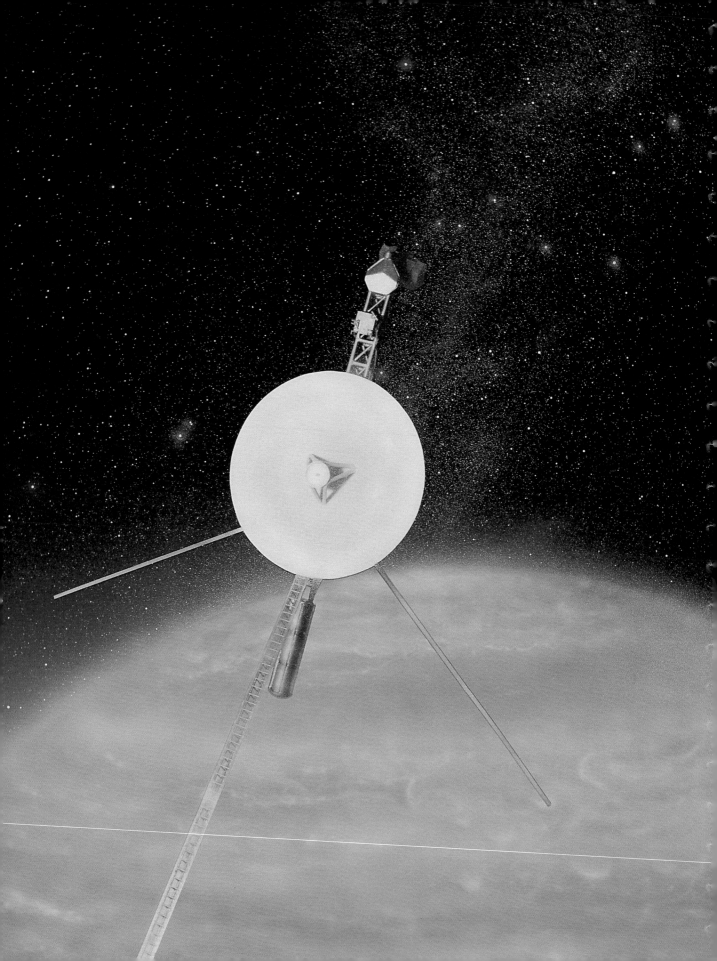

impulses that spread out like ripples in a lake. They are picked up by radio telescopes as light. Although radio galaxies are located mainly at the farthest points of the universe, their extreme energy makes them appear brighter than objects many times closer.

What Next?

Astronomers will continue to study both near and far skies in an effort to determine whether the universe will start to contract sometime in the future. And, in the meantime, they will work to better understand the pieces of the puzzle that are in place.

In addition to using space probes and satellites, astronomers will continue to view the heavens from Earth-based observatories. Their equipment, however, will be ever more sophisticated. For example, a sky mapping project is now in place at an observatory in New Mexico that is intended to map more than half the heavens in three dimensions and five colors. The atlas that will be produced will be 100 times clearer than the sky charts now available. The project team also intends to make the material available on CD-ROMs for computer use. It will take 200 discs to contain this new view of the skies—a view that, even 50 years ago, was unimaginable.

A Closer Look

Look at the map of Mars on page 46. If you were choosing a spot on which to land a space probe, where would it be? Why? Do some research in the library or on the Internet and find out where the 1997 Mars *Pathfinder* probe landed. What was the surface like? Was it flat or hilly? Which area on the map in this book looks most like Pathfinder's landing spot?

Glossary

Big Bang The explosion of energy that was the origin of the universe.

black hole A gravitational field that is so strong nothing can escape it, even light.

Coriolis Effect The effect of the rotation of Earth on wind direction.

doldrums An area in the ocean near the equator where winds blow only very lightly or not at all.

easterlies Winds that blow east to west between 60 degrees north and south latitude and the poles.

gyre An enormous and powerful circular flow pattern formed by interconnecting ocean currents.

isotherm A line on a map that connects points with the same temperature.

manganese nodule A mineral-rich, potato-shaped lump found on the ocean floor.

meteor A meteoroid that falls into Earth's atmosphere and burns up.

meteoroid Space dust or a small rock.

moon A natural satellite that orbits a planet.

neutron star The core of a red giant star that has exploded in a supernova.

prevailing winds Winds that blow consistently from one direction.

pulsar A neutron star that spins very quickly and gives off a flash of energy with each spin.

quasar A star-like object about the size of our solar system, but with the mass of an entire galaxy.

radio galaxy A galaxy that gives off extremely powerful radio waves, which are a form of radiation.

red giant A dying star swollen many times its original size.

seamount A towering underwater mountain.

sonar A system that uses reflected sound waves to locate objects.

supernova An explosion of a red giant star.

trade winds Winds that blow from the equator to 30 degrees north latitude and 30 degrees south latitude.

trench A very deep, narrow valley in the ocean floor.

tsunami A huge wave caused by underwater earthquakes or eruptions.

westerlies Winds that blow west to east between 30 and 60 degrees north and south latitude.

white dwarf The hot core remaining when a red giant collapses.

Further Reading

Atkinson, Stuart. *Astronomy*. London, England: Usborne Publishing Ltd., 1994

Barnes-Svarney, Patricia. *Traveler's Guide to the Solar System*. New York, NY: Sterling Publishing Co., Inc., 1993

Couper, Heather and Nigel Henbest. *Big Bang*. New York: DK Publishing, 1997

The Encyclopedia of Space Travel and Astronomy. New York: Octopus Books Limited, 1985

Ganeri, Anita. *The Oceans Atlas*. New York: Dorling Kindersley, Inc., 1994

Kaufman, Joe. *Joe Kaufman's Big Book about Earth and Space*. New York: Western Publishing Company, Inc., 1987

Lambert, David. *The Kingfisher Young People's Book of Oceans*. New York: Kingfisher, 1997

———— *Seas and Oceans*. Morristown, NJ: Silver Burdett Press, 1987

Mosley, John. *The Ultimate Guide to the Sky*. Los Angeles: RGA Publishing Group, Inc., 1997

Ridpath, Ian. *Facts on File: Stars and Planets Atlas*. London, England: George Phillip Limited, 1997

Simon, Seymour. *Space Words: A Dictionary*. New York: Harper Collins, 1991

Talbot, Frank H. *Under the Sea*. San Francisco: Weldon Owen Reference, Inc., 1995

Voss, Gilbert L. *Oceanography*. New York: Western Publishing Company, Inc., 1972

Index

Page numbers for illustrations are in boldface.